DARE TO TRUST GOD'S WORD

THE FOUNDATION OF ALL HOPE

LELA BURBRIDGE

CONTENTS

To my family and friends, you are the rays of sunshine God has put in my path to remind me of His love and faithfulness.

INTRODUCTION

L ife is not always smooth sailing, there will always be storms looming over the horizon and our faith may waver under the strain. But we need to remember Jesus is in the boat with us. If we dare to trust God's Word as the foundation of hope, we will thrive.

I cannot have been much older than a toddler when my mother gave me away to another. In retrospect I often marvel at her strength to do so and I cannot begin to imagine the desperation she must have faced. It breaks my heart to tell you that those to whom I was entrusted proved unfit to be called my guardians. My early years were filled with cruelty, neglect and abuse. Eventually, when I could not endure it anymore, I escaped onto the unforgiving streets of Kampala. Still only a young child; vulnerable and totally alone in the world. In time, through the kindness of others, I came to reunite with my true family; only for jealousy and murder to throw us into a life of desperation and poverty. The scourge of HIV/AIDs tore through our world and death swiftly followed. And so, at the tender age of twelve I found myself the head of my family, denied a guardian of my own once more. By God's grace I endured; through trusting Him and by sheer determination for a better future I fought to survive.

Growing up, poverty weighed heavily and disease took many from me. I was then stigmatised for my trauma, as those with whom I tried to seek solace with would often reject me. Harrowing memories of these times would haunt me in the depth of the night. And yet I can testify of the love of God. I fought against the adversities the world threw at me to gain an education. I am a child no longer; I walk as a woman in faith, now a mother to three precious children and wife to an extraordinary husband. The Lord has been faithful. I stand in awe at how far I have come, but the contrast is very difficult for me to adjust to, it feels almost like a contradiction.

This spurred me on to write a chronicle of my childhood in Uganda, *Lela: Ashes of Childhood*. I was determined that the storms I had passed through should be turned to positive use. But my fear was that, upon reading the book, those who knew me would see me differently. I was so scared that once they uncovered the truth of who I really was, they would look upon me in judgment and I would face rejection once again. In reality, I was met with overwhelming kindness and love. Many questioned how I had the strength to persevere. How could I now be so full of hope given all that I had gone through? I was inspired by these responses to write this devotional as a testimony to the true source of my strength and hope: God's Word.

This book is not intended to wholly represent all that I am. I simply want to give space to explore my perspective and begin the process of unpacking my journey of faith as a Christian.

This devotional is split into two parts: the first part is intended to encourage you to trust God in situations that may seem impossible; the second part explores how we ought to aspire to live as followers of Jesus in our daily life.

The Bible passages quoted throughout this book were chosen as they have had a profound impact on my life. They have sustained me and I have taken them to heart. In times of trouble and need I return to them again and again. When I wrestle with God in prayer, as Jacob does in the book of Genesis (Gen. 32:22-32), I remind God of His promises found within His Word, the foundation of all hope.

PART ONE

Trusting Even When it is Hard

1

THE DESERT PLACE

*They did not thirst when he led them through
the deserts; he made water flow for them from
the rock; he split the rock and water gushed out.
(Isaiah 48:21)*

Throughout my life the Word of God has been a
refuge in times of despair. The troubles that plague
our hearts grow by the day and it is becoming
increasingly difficult to have hope. For those who have
faith in God, our faith is tested at every turn. Often, as fresh
tests arise, there are times where we may not be standing
in faith. For me, life without God is dry and hopeless; a
desert place.

Not so long ago, I faced the possibility of being
separated from my husband and children. I had lived
in England for more than eleven years by this point, my
foster parents having brought me back with them from

their time of mission in Uganda in order that I could have access to further education. I had since married Andrew and the time had come, after five years of marriage, to finalise an application for settlement in the United Kingdom. I was at my most vulnerable, pregnant with my third child; it was to be an incredibly difficult time. Both my husband and I were self-employed and I was beginning to settle down in preparation for the baby. Even though we did not have much, with bills to pay and two other small children to care for, we were still able to make ends meet. I believe it is the most basic human right to be permitted to live in the country your husband and children are citizens of. A family should be free to live together in peace. But it was a time when the country required us to prove that children needed their mother and a husband needed his wife.

The settlement application was well prepared even before I booked the appointment with the Home Office. Having spent many years in the country as a student I had learned to navigate the intricate maze of the visa system. Once every couple of years every inch of my existence would be examined, cross-examined and accounted for. I would have to spend too many late nights in the months leading up to an application compiling a huge folder of evidence and documents.

I prayed ceaselessly during this time, trusting God to help me remember everything I needed to. The appointment was in Cardiff; the pleasant demeanour of a small Welsh office was a far more appealing prospect than the sprawling Home Office centres in London. Given we were going all the way to Wales, we decided to fit in a family holiday. What could go wrong? We started looking for accommodation. However, the more I prayed, the more my unease grew. Perhaps it would be better to hold off planning the holiday until after the appointment? What we did not know was that God had already gone ahead of us – He already knew the outcome.

The big day arrived. By now I was six months pregnant. After climbing the stairs to the visa office I was already exhausted. The wait while my application was processed seemed to take forever and the children were becoming increasingly bored and hungry. I had brought my little family with me as I could not bear to face this alone; keeping my husband and children close helped immeasurably to keep my anxiety in check.

After four long hours we were called forward. I remember wondering, 'Why had it taken so long?' and I was completely unprepared for the news we were about to get. My application had not even been considered; it had taken four hours to get to that conclusion! The caseworker explained that although all the information we had given was correct and well organised, they had turned us down because I applied 21 days too early. The £3000 we had paid for this would not be refunded. Gobsmacked, I objected for I had only applied at that time on the very advice of the Home Office. I pleaded with them that I had done everything right, could they not see this? It became clear that we were set up to fail. At that moment, Andrew and I went into panic mode.

A seemingly small mistake was enough to change the course of our life irreversibly. What were we going to do? We did not have much money and the little we did have would endlessly go towards more visas. The cycle of extraordinarily expensive rubber-stamped pieces of paper would continue with no end in sight. It was so frustrating!

I was crying uncontrollably, constantly muttering and telling God I did not know what to do. But then suddenly I became calm and peace came upon me. I could not explain it other than to say that God had heard my cries. In that moment I knew His presence was there with us. I embraced my husband and my startled children, reassuring them that it was going to be OK. It can only be God who gave me that strength in that moment.

The caseworker's supervisor came in and said there was nothing that could be done. They informed us that we should go back to the beginning of the whole process and reapply. We rejected this out of hand and asked for a moment to think. But then, a miracle: the supervisor came to us in the corridor and pulled us to one side. He would offer to open up another appointment, but only if we could pay a further £3000 on the spot. Leaving the secure office without immediately accepting this, we would have no way of reaching him and absolutely no guarantee of booking a second interview within the right time frame. Stunned at this offer, it confirmed to me that God had heard me and was there with us. We should trust that although this path was narrow, it was the right one to take.

We were able to scramble the money together and book another date, but it did not give us much comfort. We returned home feeling utterly cold and hopeless, our faith was being severely tested. We were deeply frightened at the prospect of unwittingly repeating the same outcome. Weak and dismayed we allowed doubt to creep in. We sought advice to find out if anything else could be done and spoke to an immigration lawyer about what had happened. Her jaw dropped; they had given us another appointment on the spot! She couldn't believe it, because it never happens, it was impossible. Through this situation I experienced God's grace first-hand. You see, I serve the God of the impossible.

Although I often cried, I also knew that it was important to trust God through those three weeks we had to wait. We consulted another lawyer through friends; he advised us to call the Home Office and pull all our documents, as he was convinced that they would not grant the settlement. But I held steadfast and refused to take this advice; I knew that my God was in control. Still though, the question of whether I was making the right decision plagued me and I would cry out to God in frustration.

When you find yourself in the desert place, remember that God knows your situation; He is ready to help you if you just reach out, speak to Him and ask for help. I remember reaching a point when I no longer had any words to say; I did not know how to ask for help from

God. I had the Bible close to me and I remember opening it and my eyes landing on this passage:

> But if we hope for what we do not yet have, we wait for it patiently. In the same way, the Spirit helps us in our weakness. We do not know what we ought to pray for, but the Spirit himself intercedes for us with groans that words cannot express. And he who searches our hearts knows the mind of the Spirit, because the Spirit intercedes for the saints in accordance with God's will. And we know that in all things God works for the good of those who love him, who have been called according to his purpose… What, then, shall we say in response to this? If God is for us, who can be against us?
>
> (Romans 8:25–28, 31)

As I repeatedly read these verses, it all began to sink in. God is the Father; His Son is Jesus Christ who died for the sins of all upon a cross. When Jesus rose from the dead, He went up to heaven, but left His Spirit to live in us. Knowing that God's Spirit lives in me, I appealed to Him to help me know that He is near and I asked him to keep me calm.

One day, not long after, something very strange happened to me. During this time, I would try to protect my children from my anguish and so standing in the shower became my refuge, a place I could let my tears flow. But this time, instead of crying, I felt unshackled and suddenly a heavenly language flowed out of me like a river. Euphoria overwhelmed me and I suddenly found myself laughing. When I got out of the shower I was emotionally exhausted but brighter in myself and with my hope restored. This was the Spirit of God in me, and it was so beautiful.

I believe I had spoken in tongues, which is a gift of the Spirit (see 1 Cor. 14:1–2). It was a precious moment and it confirmed to me that God knew I was weak. Though doubt and worry still afflicted me, I was able to rest in the knowledge that God was in control.

Three weeks passed and the time came to return to the Home Office in Wales. Within minutes of arriving we were told that my caseworker had already come to a decision. I was called forward and told that my application had been granted. The years of uncertainty were over! I wept with joy and felt my faith renewed in every part of me. I was free of having to justify staying with my family; free finally to live in peace.

This experience taught me that it is the hard times – when we have nowhere else to turn – that push us closer to God. The Bible tells us that when God's people were thirsty in the desert, it was then that God provided water from the rock. When we pass through the wilderness in life and we believe there is no way out, it is in these moments that our relationship with Him truly flourishes.

I was also encouraged by the story of David in the Bible. As a boy he was promised by God to be king, but then the world changed around him. It took years of him wandering in his desert place, but he never lost faith in God's promise. Even when David saw opportunities to take matters into his own hands, he refused to and chose to let God fix it for him instead. He actively trusted that as God had chosen him, God would fight for him. This was by no means easy. He poured out his heart many times as demonstrated by his writing in the book of Psalms.

When God's plan for us comes to pass, regardless of the circumstances, our human understanding is challenged. We realise that God's ways are far above ours. I encourage you to trust in the Lord in the desert place and He will not let you down. God will fulfil His purpose for your life for good; He did not deliver David into the hands of Saul. God had a purpose for David, He had chosen him, and Saul knew this. God has chosen you too which means His has a purpose for your life and it will be fulfilled (see Ps. 57:2).

The desert place that you may be walking through today is so God may refine your spirit and prepare you for even greater triumphs that will surpass your imagination.

I pray that you will find strength in your desert place as you read His Word. May you trust Him to help you find your way through as the Holy Spirit intercedes on your behalf in moments when you no longer know what to say.

2

LOVE HEALS FEAR

There is no fear in love. But perfect love drives
out fear, because fear has to do with punishment.
The one who fears is not made perfect in love.
(1 John 4:18)

When I was a young girl of about six years old I overheard my auntie, who I thought was my mother, arguing with her husband about me. I heard her shout, 'Lela is not my daughter, and she is a bastard!' I apologise for repeating such strong language, but I am exposing the impact that word had on me. Hearing someone I believed to be my mother disown me so thoroughly shattered my world. I questioned my very existence and started wondering who I was. I was afraid. All I now clearly understood was that I was unwanted but I had nowhere else to go.

After eventually escaping from my auntie, I was around eight years old when I was finally reunited with my birth mother. But, miserably, all my expectations of being loved were swiftly crushed. Although she wasn't cruel to me as my auntie was, it was clear that she saw me as an extra burden over and above what she already had to carry. Perhaps she was so thoroughly scarred from having to let me go as a baby; I imagine it left her unable to emotionally reconnect with me. Mercifully, the man she had married was a truly kind man. He cared for his stepchildren as if they were his own. It is with a heavy heart that I tell you that, a few months later, his best friend in a fit of jealousy murdered this lovely man. My mother was left an utterly broken woman.

In desperation my mother remarried. This new stepfather was not at all worthy of the title. In contrast to the last, he was vindictive and intensely cruel to my siblings and me; the aftermath of his attacks consuming us with fear. We would desperately try and protect our mother from the abuse he inflicted. All this time I had longed to be loved and accepted – but now this seemed to be only a foolish fantasy.

Being exposed to so much fear at such a tender age, my heart inevitably turned to distrust. My understanding of love became doing what I was told regardless of whether it was right or wrong. The psychological torment of this haunted me for many years, well into adulthood. I struggled so much with being able to love and receive it, that later in life I purposefully tried to push away those who tried to show me love.

I remember the time when, as a teenager studying in England, I was helping my foster father assemble a new bed. I had a small kitchen knife, which I was using to cut the plastic cover off the mattress. In a flash, quite clumsily, I slipped and the knife went straight into my foster father's hand. Seeing blood in that moment I thought it was all over for me. Surely he was going to beat me like my auntie used to. I was certain in my mind that they would cancel my stay and immediately fly me back to Uganda. I was blind with panic. In an instant and without a word said, I sprinted out of the bedroom, down the stairs, out of the house and into the night. All I could think to do was to hide among the trees in the garden. Torchlight swiftly followed the path of my hasty escape, and though I tried my best to crouch out of sight, my foster parents soon came upon my hiding place. To my amazement they met my state of shock with gentleness and understanding. They both simply embraced me and kissed me on my forehead. They calmed me down and reassured me that it was an accident, all was well, and I was not to worry. They eventually convinced me to return to the house and slowly led me in a daze back into the warmth. Words can't express how healing their response was to my fear. I had never experienced tenderness and compassion like it before. I knew I had a long way in understanding how to love, but that was a beautiful way to start.

The challenge was in understanding what real love was. I would search the Bible, praying that God would teach me about love. I came across the story of when a man asked Jesus what he could do to receive eternal life. Jesus' answer was startlingly simple and one that changed my entire outlook on life. He said, "'Love the Lord your God with all your heart and with all your soul and with all your strength and with all your mind"; and, "Love your neighbour as yourself'" (Lk. 10:27). I finally understood that to love, I had to love God first with everything I had. I then made a decision to put others first and love without judgment. Devotion to the Word of God on a personal level flooded me with profound understanding, and slowly, through much patience, I worked on how to love myself too.

Meeting my husband was the turning point in my life where I fully understood the meaning of love. I came to understand clearly what loving others really meant. Love is accepting fully despite our weaknesses. Love is not merely a fleeting feeling; love is a continuous and active choice.

In previous romantic relationships, every time I shared my past there would follow awkward excuses from the man about why we should not be together, or his communication would abruptly stop, and interest in me vanish. One day, very early on in our relationship, Andrew gave me a lift home. It was a summer evening in the English countryside and the sky was clear and beautiful. Andrew suggested that before he dropped me back home, we could continue to the old airfield to star gaze a little together. We sat side by side on the bonnet in silence; the cool breeze rustling the long meadow the only sound.

I felt a sudden sense of security and I decided it was now or never; it was time I opened up to him. I told him about my past; unveiling all that I had been withholding. The many scars and traumas I carried now revealed. Shaking a little, I looked up at him; a feeling of shame crept up my neck. Not saying a word, he cast no judgment; he simply met my eyes and just held me close. What felt like an eternity passed in those minutes; it was getting late so we got back into the car and he took me home. At the door he kissed me goodnight and drove off.

I kicked myself as I walked up the stairs to my bed. 'How stupid was that?' I asked myself. 'I should have kept my mouth shut. I have just ruined my only chance to go out with a handsome, kind and godly young man'. I consoled myself, 'Oh well, he is not the first one to disappear after hearing all that and, I guess, unlikely to be the last; I better just get used to it.'

After a restless night, in the morning my phone buzzed: he wanted to see me! This isn't how this normally goes; surely he just wants to be polite and let me down gently? Andrew returned and offered to take me out to a restaurant, and apprehensively I accepted the invitation. When we arrived, although I was hungry, I simply was unable to eat. I was so on edge just waiting for that moment he would explain why we could not be together. He noticed my full plate and asked why I was not eating. Did I not like the food? I replied that the butterflies in my stomach were overwhelming. He laughed, and with a smile offered quite selflessly to finish my plate as well.

As we continued talking, he asked whether I would mind being introduced to his family: would I join him at his parents' 30th wedding anniversary? Shocked, I burst out 'Yes!' Although confused at this unprecedented turn of events, all the fear within me evaporated. The butterflies in my stomach, however, went crazy!

As our relationship grew, we prayed and read God's Word together. I tried my usual methods of pushing people away, but none worked on him. There is no denying that he loved me and wanted to be with me, despite all of my imperfections. He was so accepting, gentle and patient. I suddenly understood what God's Word meant when it said, 'There is no fear in love. But perfect love drives out fear, because fear has to do with punishment' (1 Jn. 4:18).

I had been so afraid that I would be rejected but Andrew's gentleness reassured me of his love. I can confidently say that true love based on the Word of God really does heal feelings of rejection. I could not believe someone could actually love me with all my baggage and self-pity. This man's love reminded me of God's love for all of us. It does not matter what your past has been, God is ready to love you if you allow Him in.

We do not have to look far for love. Look at the people God has put in your life. Despite the lack of love in my childhood, I now know that there are those who go the extra mile to accept you for who you are. There are those who are there for you in your hour of need. They do not have to be, but they choose to; because they love you. There was the kindness of the English lady whom I met as a stranger at a Joyce Meyer crusade in Uganda. I was inexplicably drawn to her, but she did not meet me, then a street child, with rejection when I approached her. She saw beyond the surface and without question she took my hand and accepted me as I was. I call that unconditional love. She would later lead me to meet my foster parents, who would in turn open the door to further education for me. She gifted me new hope.

I have learned that love is a two-way street: where you don't just receive, but also give. God our Father loves us so much and He hopes we love Him back; expressing this through our attitudes and actions.

I pray that when you feel hurt and cast down you will look to God. Can you see how beautifully He created you? You are His masterpiece. He loves you so much that He made everything about you unique. Discover true love as you read God's Word. As God loves you, I pray that you will be able to, with God's help, love yourself and that His love would replace all those feelings of rejection. As you look around you, it is my prayer that you will see and appreciate the good things God has blessed you with. I pray that this may bring you healing.

3

EMBRACING REJECTION

For the LORD will not reject his people; he will
never forsake his inheritance. (Psalm 94:14)

We all experience and react to rejection in different ways. Often, we are only able to cope by being resentful or holding a grudge towards the people who hurt us. Sometimes, this is the case because we have not embraced and accepted the events in the way they transpired. As such, we live in denial and so we are unable to move on from the negative experience. Accepting the reality of your rejection is the very first step that you must take in order to move on from hurtful experiences.

Rejection is one of the most unpleasant feelings that you can ever know in life. The rejection that Jesus Christ suffered at the hands of those He came to save was too much for anyone to bear; yet our LORD endured it for our sake. He took your place and my place of suffering, rejection and humiliation.

For me, rejection began with my mother. With no other option, and in a place of desperation she painfully gave me up as a baby; then those very people she had entrusted me with systematically afflicted abuse on me. A small child rejected by those I believed to be my own family. But I tell you that even at that time of suffering, even before I heard of Him, God was with me and He had a plan for *me*.

I asked for forgiveness and received Jesus Christ as my Lord and personal Saviour when I was about nine years old. Now, you may ask how I could have such assurance and certainty at that tender age? I would probably not have a satisfying answer for you. What I can say is that life did not change for me straight away. I still struggled. So, no: I had no deep understanding of what I had just affirmed; nor did I understand the gravity of the choice. But the words of Jesus that I heard that day had a most profound effect on me that I have not come close to experiencing since, "'Let the little children come to me, and do not hinder them, for the kingdom of heaven belongs to such as these'" (Mt. 19:14).

These words echoed across a dusty Kampala street where a throng of children had gathered. I was passing by, on my regular errand to buy milk as a salve for my stepfather's hangover. Curious and frankly open to distraction from my task, I approached the crowd and saw a man in a smart suit speaking out with a sweet, genuine tone. These words struck me like a lightning bolt to the heart. Even at such a young age, the verses resonated. I had yearned to belong. To be told that there was a Kingdom that was mine, a Kingdom that not only accepted everyone regardless of age, but also lifted them and granted them true significance. I cannot express how comforted I was by these words. This was the God who *recognised* me, *welcomed* me, *created* me, and has a *plan* for my future. I was neither forgotten nor unwanted.

And yet, my life continued from this point in the same sequence as before I became a Christian. I was still unloved by the ones around me and continued to live in abject poverty. Despite being reunited with my true mother, my quality of life did not improve. We moved into one of the worst slums in Uganda. A one-room tin shack served as our home. There was a hole cut crudely out of the iron that functioned as our solitary window. We lacked beds and had no flooring to speak of so slept huddled together in the dust. At night, we looked like sardines in a can. So many times we went without food, we had no clothes other than the little we wore and our feet were bare. Getting an education was now an unattainable dream and we stopped going to school.

Although I faced this hardship, there was a marked difference in the way I experienced and perceived my surroundings. I became more accepting of my situation and the more rejection I experienced, the more resilient I became and was able to handle every hardship that life threw at me. I did this knowing and trusting that God was with me.

Rejections came in various forms during my life while growing up. I was not impervious to crushes. You see, I was so driven to get an education I began doing odd jobs for people. I worked at everything from washing clothes to cleaning houses and cooking, even though it paid very poorly and absorbed most of my energy working until late at night. With this little money I would convince a school I had a sponsor and enrol myself. I was constantly on edge. Would they find out the truth? When the time came round to pay the term fees I would sneak out and disappear. Again I would raise money in whatever way I could and find another school to begin the cycle over. Eventually there was one headmaster who, though seeing through my scheme, took pity on me. He appreciated my determination and permitted me to stay in class for a full year, waiving my fees. It was while at this school that I was finally able to let my guard down and truly be a teenager for the first time.

Feelings of attraction can be very cruel at times, because you cannot control how and with whom you fall in love. There was a particularly painful experience, which I believe many of my readers may identify with from their own adolescence. There was a boy in my secondary school; very handsome and clever (or at least I thought he was at the time). I wanted to be his friend and I would do anything for him to notice me. But at the same time, I knew I was not in his league. I came from a poor family; my worn clothes betrayed me, hanging loosely off my bones. I had often skipped meals at school due to lack of money. Yet I was determined. I would look for any opportunity I could and would even offer to carry his bag or pick up his books for him.

I am sure he saw straight through my designs and my girlfriends would often tease me about him. One of them even dared me to tell him how I felt so I wrote him a letter. I went to the shop and bought one sheet of paper from a notepad and a fountain pen for 500 shillings. I wanted it to be special, so the paper I chose was pink with roses and hearts on it. I guess he was very polite to reply at all. He informed me that he did not think I was his type, and just to be clear he bluntly added that it was due to the way I looked. My face burned with embarrassment and I felt totally ashamed of myself.

Looking back at this episode as an adult, it is more amusing for me than anything else. However, I still consider the effect it had on my teenage self-esteem. I suddenly felt humiliated, far from beautiful and inadequate. This took a toll on my schoolwork and social life. It would have been even more draining if I had not known what the Word of God said about me, 'I praise you because I am fearfully and wonderfully made' (Ps. 139:14).

These words helped me to accept that I am the work of miraculous hands. It was the Lord who formed me; I am valuable in His eyes because I am part of His handiwork and, therefore, I am beautiful by His assessment. Despite how I was feeling at that time, I had to trust what God's Word says about me and to carry on with the assurance of Him by my side.

These experiences and the understanding to turn always to God's Word for guidance and inspiration strengthened my resolve and focus in the critical years of my transition from childhood to adulthood. Even though I struggled to make sense of most of these experiences of rejection, I made a choice to deal with them positively by embracing the reality of who I am in God's eyes. The testing experiences could then yield opportunity for meaningful lessons that would influence and enrich the rest of my life. I have learnt that rejection can be healed by the love of God. When we feel alone, the love of God is closer, and His Word assures us of this, 'How priceless is your unfailing love! Both high and low among men find refuge in the shadow of your wings' (Ps. 36:7).

It is my prayer that you will take refuge under the wings of God. That you will trust Him when life seems unbearable and when you feel exhausted and weary. I pray that you will sense His presence close to you and you will let Him comfort you.

4

THE PAST IN THE PRESENT

Trust in the LORD *with all your heart and lean
not on your own understanding; in all your
ways acknowledge him, and he will make your
paths straight. (Proverbs 3:5–6)*

For most parents having a child is a happy event. Well, for me, having a child brings to the surface a whole host of intense emotions. Each time I have had a baby, the past returns to me and I overflow with anxiety. The thought that something bad might happen to my newborn child dominates my mind.

When I was a young girl of about eleven or twelve, my mother passed away. HIV/AIDS stole her from me. I suddenly found myself on the streets; the sole provider and protector of my siblings. Before long the youngest and most vulnerable of us, my baby sister, became ill. We rushed her to the hospital, but as we had no money, we only had hope of charity. When we arrived, the doctors refused even to look at her unless we paid. I will never forget standing in the queue for almost five hours, pleading for help, holding her in my arms until she took her last breath.

This trauma from my past is very active in my present. With each of my own new babies I have found myself overwhelmingly anxious and confused. Any time my baby would cry, even without cause, I was blinded by panic. Even with the reassurance of now living in a country with an accessible and reliable health system, I was incapable of relaxing with my little one. I found myself unable to sleep, utterly fixated on monitoring their breathing through the long nights.

When my baby sister was born, she was so little but so beautiful; it's strange but despite our circumstances she never cried. The strongest of all my memories was the way you could always rely on her for a smile, her eyes so tender and kind. She was a blessing that came to us when things were very difficult; a ray of light in the darkest of times. Yet her father (my stepfather) refused to recognise her as his child. In his twisted mind she only represented his new wife's failure to provide him with a son. And so, shortly after my mother succumbed to her sickness, I was left as the primary carer, the eldest daughter aged twelve, alongside my aged and frail grandmother.

For years I was incapable of talking about my baby sister. It was not until I had a child of my own that things began to change. Suddenly, all my raw memories of her came flooding back to me. I was terrified of telling anyone in case they thought I was losing my marbles. It was through prayer that God gave me the wisdom to recognise that my past was taking control of my present. I turned to God's Word – I could not afford to let my past strangle my present and future. I called upon my closest friends from my church family and together we prayed.

Grief is a strange thing, especially when you come from a culture where life seems so cheap; where there is so little time to properly process a loss, especially for a child. When my mother died, instead of grieving for her I became the head of the family. There was not a moment free to reflect on what had just happened. When my sister died, there was no time to grieve for her either; I could only concentrate on trying to survive and my other remaining younger siblings.

Not knowing how to grieve was the single most painful thing about losing my mother and my sister. I was always filled with fear that they were gone forever. The only way I could remember them was looking back at their final moments when they were put in the ground and covered with soil. I didn't like these images at all; they disturbed me.

I thought all this would pass and I would soon forget about them, but the love I had for them was too deep. I needed to keep their memories alive, but I was alone and had no one to share them with. I longed to be asked about my loss or how I felt. I remember a time when a kind lady gifted me clothes. I was so grateful to receive them but then I overheard her daughter whisper 'Mummy, why do you give my old clothes to that girl?' Her mother simply replied, 'Darling, she is an orphan'. My heart sank, the label stung, it had never occurred to me before that this was what I was now. 'Orphan' was a term which came to dominate my identity, and I loathed it for disregarding my mother and I took it to be an ugly profanity. But I was too scared to tell people that I didn't like it. I would feel too guilty because those who used it most were so often the very ones trying to help me.

I was so angry with God for letting me go through these ordeals. I wanted to remain bitter but the more I thought about it, I realised that it only hindered me from moving forward. So, one day, I made the decision not to be defined by my past. Yes, I was orphaned, but that did not mean I should dwell on it and let my whole existence be one of sorrow. I decided to use my past to positively open doors: to put others before myself and seek to guide them onto a better path. I must say that this was not an overnight success. I spent many midnight hours submitting myself to God, praying through tears of anguish, 'let my story not be one of bitterness, let it be one of giving hope'.

It was only through the Word of God that I was able to deal with all this loss and to find comfort. It is through the Bible that God speaks to us His Word. I realised that I was alive and well for a reason; I have been able to remain strong through it all because God *was* and *is* with me, 'Blessed are those who mourn, for they will be comforted' (Mt. 5:4).

It was only then that I gave myself permission to mourn my loss. I went for a walk and found a peaceful meadow in the countryside. I sat amongst the waving grass and wildflowers and gripped my Bible. Finally, in that moment I allowed God to set me free, and I wept. For the first time I did not want to be comforted by any human; it was something I had to do by myself with my Creator. It was as if God and I opened a new line of communication. I realised that my relationship with Him was a personal one, and I could talk to Him directly anytime just as He could talk to me through the Bible, creation, friends, to name a few. He is, after all, my Father. The voice of God in that moment was not like the physical voice of a friend – it was something miraculous; something divine. Now, you may be thinking, surely such miracles were reserved for biblical times. Yet I say to you that this moment was quite simply extraordinary; holy in a way that defies my capability to describe in words. And as a heavenly peace descended upon me, I knew He had heard me.

While reading the Bible, God's Word, I stumbled upon this passage, and found comfort.

> Brothers, we do not want you to be ignorant about those who fall asleep, or to grieve like the rest of men, who have no hope. We believe that Jesus died and rose again and so we believe that

God will bring with Jesus those who have fallen asleep in him. According to the Lord's own word, we tell you that we who are still alive, who are left till the coming of the Lord, will certainly not precede those who have fallen asleep. For the Lord himself will come down from heaven, with a loud command, with the voice of the archangel and with the trumpet call of God, and the dead in Christ will rise first. After that, we who are still alive and are left will be caught up together with them in the clouds to meet the Lord in the air. And so we will be with the Lord for ever. Therefore encourage each other with these words.

(1 Thessalonians 4:13–18)

God had reassured me with a promise that I would see my loved ones again. And so, I chose to remember my little sister's beautiful smile. I forgave my mother and chose to remember her only by her love. This does not mean I forget what had occurred, but I want to enjoy my present and embrace the future with confidence with my God beside me. To do this though, I must be positive and seek to help others to honour their past in their present, however difficult it may have been.

My past was extraordinarily difficult. But I know that I am a child of God and that His Word tells me that He has good plans for my future. I shouldn't be anxious about anything because the God who created the Universe has spoken over me. I choose to trust His Word despite not forgetting the toils of yesterday. I look forward to a bright tomorrow because He is carrying me through.

It is my prayer, therefore, that sharing my past with you will encourage you to move forward in life with confidence, trusting that God is with you. I pray that you will trust Him with everything you are and believe that He will always direct your path with wisdom.

5

FEELINGS OF ANXIETY

When anxiety was great within me, your
consolation brought joy to my soul. (Psalm 94:19)

Anxiety is one of those emotions that is so tempting to suffer in silence as an inner turmoil. We might find ourselves too ashamed and embarrassed to talk about it with others. We are afraid of being judged and that others may consider us to be less 'Christian'. It is entirely normal to feel like this; so many other Christians around the world experience these same feelings. God wants us to trust Him in times when we feel vulnerable, confused, scared and out of control.

I never really understood how frightening anxiety could be until I had my first child. After she was born, I suddenly began feeling anxious about everything. I was worried something bad was going to happen to my child or to me. I think I also suffered mildly from postnatal depression but I was too terrified to tell anyone, even my husband. I was afraid my baby would be taken away. I was afraid of what people at church would think; I was afraid of losing control and not being able to cope with a new baby on my own.

I prayed through tears begging God to take away all these feelings of anxiety. I felt ungodly to feel this way. I constantly rebuked the feeling, but that did not help. I slipped into exhaustion and desperation. In all of this, I never stopped to explore what the Word of God says about feeling anxious.

Eventually, when all else seemed to fail, in desperation I turned to Scripture. I wanted to know if anyone in the Bible had ever felt or experienced any form of anxiety and depression. So, I started from the beginning. I was encouraged when I read stories like that of Noah and the Ark in Genesis. I cannot begin to imagine the depression Noah must have suffered, to know that all these people were going to perish because of their stubbornness. Equally, he must have been very anxious about the floods coming but we see him faithfully obeying all of God's instructions and trusting every word.

I read about how when Jesus was about to hand himself over to his enemies He pleaded with God, His Father, "'My soul is overwhelmed with sorrow to the point of death… My Father, if it is possible, may this cup be taken from me'" (Mt. 26:38–39). This made me consider that even the Son of God Himself felt intensely vulnerable. He had all the power to stop death and yet chose to suffer by dying for our sins, and the stress of this act caused him to sweat like he was bleeding in the Garden of Gethsemane. He demonstrated that, even in the greatest fear, we can trust and rest in God. In Luke's account of this precise moment we see God send an angel to strengthen Jesus: 'An angel from heaven appeared to him and strengthened him. And being in anguish, he prayed more earnestly, and his sweat was like drops of blood falling to the ground' (Lk. 22:43–44).

With prayer I started to share my feelings with those close to me and I asked them to pray for me and with me. I remember speaking to one of my fellow mum friends explaining how some days I did not feel like getting out of bed, how I struggled to bond with my baby, and how scared I was of not being in control. Her response surprised me; she put her arm around me and started to cry. She felt sorry for me but also explained that she had felt anxious for so long that she had to seek medical help. She had been on medication, which was helping her. It made me feel encouraged, understood and not alone.

I shared with more people and I then realised that everyone I told wanted me to feel better. They all wanted me to know that they cared and that surprised and encouraged me. I talked with my health visitor who assured me that it was not uncommon for women with new babies to feel this way. On hearing this I was very surprised because no one I knew at the time had ever talked about it.

I realised I came from a culture where women really never had a chance to talk about feelings of anxiety or depression. It was not socially acceptable conversation. I also remembered that there would be lots of family and friends around when you became a new mother in Uganda. I thought of the time when a neighbour's daughter returned to her mother's house to be cared for after she gave birth. The only job that she had was to feed the baby and then the family would take the baby so she could rest. I longed for that level of support. I laughed at myself because even if I managed to go to Uganda with my baby, I had no mother to look after me, and my sisters could not afford to be of any help. These thoughts only made me sadder.

To those Christians who feel like they have something to lose by talking about anxiety and depression, I have good news for you – it's absolutely OK to open up about your struggles. No matter how long it takes you, it is important that you do the following:

- Acknowledge that you feel the way you do.
- Consult God and trust that His support is ever-present.
- Pray for courage and grace that will see you through the situation that you are in.
- Reach out to your family and loved ones because God has placed them in your life for a reason; part of that should be their unconditional support.
- Seek support from your health professionals.

Understanding why anxiety and depression manifests at certain points in our lives can be made smoother with the help of health professionals who God has gifted with knowledge. He has placed them in our paths to offer us help and support throughout the process of our healing, and we should be open to engage with their expertise as often as necessary.

Remember that God created all things. It is ultimately from Him that the knowledge of how to help others comes. It is God who gives health professionals the skills to understand medication. With prayer, we can trust that if you ask for help with anxiety and depression and your health professional feels that medication is needed, this is an option to discuss with your family.

The Word of God tells us not to lean on our own understanding but trust God (see Prov. 3:5). Therefore, I choose to trust God when I am anxious and encourage you to do so also. 'But those who hope in the LORD will renew their strength. They will soar on wings like eagles; they will run and not grow weary, they will walk and not be faint' (Is. 40:31). Read the Word of God; take comfort from the stories told in the Bible when God's servants faced hard times.

We should also remember that God has given family and friends to support us emotionally. Our church family can be of great support in times when we feel anxious and depressed. You will be surprised how many of your sisters and brothers in Christ may be going through similar emotions. By sharing your struggles in this way, God is helping you find the hope and the help you need.

It is my prayer that you may seek God in times where you feel confused, scared and overwhelmed by anxiety. May God guide you and show you how to find help, and as you open up and share your feelings, I pray that you will know peace and joy in God our refuge.

6

WHEN GOD'S ANSWER IS 'NO'

"Ask and it will be given to you; seek and you will find; knock and the door will be opened to you."
(Matthew 7:7)

At the age of fifteen, while confiding with a close friend, I recounted my sorrows of being bullied at school about my past. I spoke about how life was proving very difficult for me and how I felt I was unable to be my true self anymore. Her response to me has stayed with me ever since. She didn't say: 'Oh! Lela, stop whining!', the response I felt I duly deserved; but rather, she said to me: 'Lela, God loves you! But you have to remember that he does not promise a straight road in life.'

The sheer simplicity of this notion astounded me. Knowing her as well as I did, I knew that these words were ones that she lived by. Her complete faith and trust in

God, even when His workings were not clear, was for me a character trait worth of emulation.

Although God encourages us to approach Him boldly with our desires, it is important that we come to Him with humility. When we pray, we can fall into the trap of presuming upon a contract with God. One in which all our requests should be answered in precisely the way we imagined, as if we know best.

Don't get me wrong, God answers prayer. However, the answer we want is not always necessarily the answer we need. We should believe in miracles: the woman who had been bleeding for twelve years, who touched Jesus' cloak in a crowd, came forward in humility and was healed for her faith (see Lk. 8:43–48). It's also worth noting that God's timing is not our own. God is over all things; He is bigger than our imagination and our response should be that of faithful patience as we wait on Him. Because faith is believing without seeing directly. In order to grow an oak tree, you must first plant an acorn and have the commitment to nurture it with patience.

Often it is only in hindsight that we can understand how He has worked in our lives, which is why it is so important we examine our past with discernment. Events that seemed to work against us, may in time prove to have led us towards our hopes. This is why bitterness can be so destructive, it clouds our vision of His works. We have to remember God's ways are so much more perfect than ours and He will give us only what is right for us in accordance with His Word.

Knowing that things do not often work out as we expect them to, what do we do when God's answer to our prayer is 'no'? We should still trust God and what His Word says.

> Abraham said to God, "If only Ishmael might live under your blessing!" Then God said: "Yes, but your wife Sarah will bear you a son, and you will call him Isaac. I will establish my covenant with him as an everlasting covenant for his descendants after him. And as for Ishmael, I have heard you: I will surely bless him; … I will make him into a great nation.
>
> (Genesis 17:18–20)

God said 'no' to Abraham. God had made a promise that He would bless nations through Abraham's lineage. Abraham's prayer was that He would make Ishmael, his eldest child, the one to be blessed and carry forward his legacy. God had a different idea. Isaac, Ishmael's younger brother, was to be His chosen one. But, because God had heard Abraham's prayers for Ishmael, God decided to bless Ishmael *as well* – just in a different way.

From this story I learned that when we pray and the answer is not what we expected, it does not mean that God has not heard our prayers. God always hears us but He has His own methods and timings. Equally, we should not doubt that God will do the best for us, even if the best feels painful and confusing.

I remember praying for my mother to get better; I had so many plans for us and there were so many things I wanted to tell her, but God's answer to my prayer was 'no'. My mother died; God called her home. This was very hard to accept and I stopped praying for a while. I was furious with God. In my prayers I reminded Him of the promises He had made in His Word, 'Ask and it will be given to you' (Mt. 7:7). I had asked for Him to heal my mother, but instead He allowed her to be taken from me. Despite my pain, by God's grace I did not stop believing in Him. The promises in His Word spoke to me even then. I knew I needed to hang on to His Word in order for my hope for a better life to stay alive within me.

I still mourn the loss of my mother to this day. I miss her and sometimes I wonder how life would have been if she was still alive. I am in a position now where I would have been able to provide a safe haven for her, a home of her own. I would have brought her grandchildren to her and watched as she tickled them and told them stories by the firelight. I would have laughed at how she would spoil my husband and endure her berating me for how she did not think I was looking after him correctly.

However, if my mother had lived, my life and story would be different. I may not have escaped the poverty of the slum, received the education I did, come to England, meet my husband, nor have had the children I have. I may not have met all the people who helped me with my healing journey. However painful my loss is, I cling on to the hope that it is all part of God's purpose.

I have close family and friends for whom things have not worked out as they hoped. Marriages have fallen apart; some are still waiting for a partner to share their life with. Others have lost children, and some have suffered bad health. Of course, they feel let down and may believe that God has ignored them. It is important we don't shut ourselves off, but instead bring to God all our frustration. We should keep communication open with Him through prayer, 'And we know that in all things God works for the good of those who love him, who have been called according to his purpose' (Rom. 8:28).

Whatever it is you don't have an answer to yet, or where the answer from God has been 'no', I urge you not to give up on your hopes and dreams. Most importantly, please do not give up on God. It can be hard to trust when you feel broken and disappointed. But I promise you that God knows what you are going through and He has a plan.

I dare you to trust His Word even in the darkest times in your life. Stand firm on His promises; He will hold you strong. Remember that there is nothing God allows you to go through that He cannot help you with. Therefore, wherever you find yourself, invite God to be with you in it, and teach you about Himself through it. God says, 'When you pass through the waters, I will be with you; and when you pass through the rivers, they will not sweep over you. When you walk through the fire, you will not be burned; the flames will not set you ablaze' (Is. 43:2).

PART TWO

Living it Out

7

FREEDOM IN FORGIVENESS

*Get rid of all bitterness, rage and anger, brawling
and slander, along with every form of malice. Be
kind and compassionate to one another, forgiving
each other, just as in Christ God forgave you.
(Ephesians 4:31–32)*

How many times when those we trust hurt us, do we store our anger and hurt in our hearts instead of turning to God? The wisdom in His Word always speaks into our situation if we seek it. We stand today in the privilege of forgiveness from our sins, through the sacrifice of Jesus on the cross. We have all sinned before God but He has shown us mercy. What better way to carry on and appreciate this grace than by living it out in our interaction with others?

I have struggled in the past to forgive. However, I have seen how a single act of forgiveness can set free all those involved from the negativity, hurt and anger of the past event. When I was a teenager, although I had now been given the opportunity to go to school, the struggle continued as poverty followed me. I noticed there was a young girl in my year who skipped meals, as I often did. Seeing myself in her I took it upon myself to look out for her. I shared all I had with her. I went to my meagre little suitcase, the sum of all I owned in the world. Of the ten clothes I had I gave her half.

I shared with her details about my life – things so personal and raw – looking for empathy and also relief from the burden of carrying these things alone. I thought I had found someone who knew what it was like, someone like me: a kindred spirit. I was mistaken; she took this sensitive information shared in confidence and recklessly whispered it around.

I stopped eating the little I had been, actively starving myself. I felt betrayed and deeply sad. I became desperately isolated within the confines of the boarding school. Someone I looked at as a friend became cold and distant.

Suddenly whispers of '*Silimu*' followed me wherever I went. All those who heard the rumours that I had lost my mother to HIV/AIDS made the assumption that I too must have it. I was perceived as the walking embodiment of death and disease. If they even touched my cup they would naively believe that they could catch it from me. Thankfully, this was towards the end of my secondary education, though it continued until I left to study in England.

Once removed from the situation, I thought that I had forgiven the girl and that it was all in the past. But every time I remembered what she had done, I found myself reliving the bitterness that I felt all over again.

It was clear there was still some part of the experience that was unfinished and it was consuming my peace. I prayed fervently, asking God to help me deal with it. In the midst of my prayers, I felt a sudden urge to pick up the phone and call her – but no! This surely could not be the answer to my prayers. I thought to myself, 'She hurt me! Why on earth should I be the one to call? Why did it fall to me to reach out?' These thoughts took root in my mind. It did not matter how often I prayed, or for how long: I knew no peace.

This is a testament to why we must follow the directions that God issues to us from His Word, by His Spirit. When we pray and study the Bible, no matter how inconvenient or unpleasant it may be, we must follow God's lead. As always, I could not see the big picture from where I was. I could not make the phone call. My reward was silence and ever-increasing inner turmoil.

This state of mind continued until I came to the realisation that if God can forgive me for my wrongs, my failings, what right did I have to hold it against her? The Bible says, 'Bear with each other and forgive whatever grievances you may have against one another. Forgive as the Lord forgave you' (Col. 3:13). I could handle it no more and in an instant – and surely only by the power of the Holy Spirit – I gathered up the courage to pick up the phone.

When she heard it was me, she broke down. I was shocked. She asked for my forgiveness. Her regret was genuine and clear, saying she had long hoped and prayed that one day she could somehow atone. I told her that I had already forgiven her by God's grace. Even though she had a lot to say to me I made it clear that I was not calling to resume our friendship but only to make peace. That call was everything I needed to be truly freed from the pain of that time. I was healed of my hurt feelings and can now look back on that experience without bitter thoughts.

I have also learned that not everyone who hurts us will respond with remorse. A merciless man repeatedly and violently sexually abused me when I was seven years old. For a long time afterwards, I was extremely bitter about what had happened to me – and justly so. However, as I became an adult the feelings of bitterness began to consume me. I had a lot of health issues as a result of this abuse. My world fell away beneath me when, at a clinic appointment, I overheard a doctor casually remark that I may struggle to have children. I remember leaving overwhelmed by tears. Unable to process my anguish through the onslaught of loss, mourning a future I may be denied because of the scars of the past.

I imagined my abuser free, happy, healthy and probably not even thinking of what he had done to me.

The more I thought about it, the more I hurt. I started enquiring about the whereabouts of this man and finally tracked down an address. Determined, I turned up at his door. Just looking at him made me sick. But what was more agonising was learning that he had four beautiful daughters. I asked if he remembered who I was. With all the bravery I could muster I told him my name and reminded him of what he had done to me.

As my voice got louder, one of his little girls asked why I was yelling at her father. Looking at her face broke me; she was a reminder of me at the age her father abused me. No matter how much I wanted to hurt this man, I knew this little girl should not have to pay for her father's wrongs. I held her face, I apologised for shouting and explained that I was asking her daddy to keep her safe. The Bible tells us 'Do not repay anyone evil for evil' (Rom. 12:17) and instructs us not to take revenge but rather leave it to God's wrath (see Rom. 12:19–21).

In honesty, in that moment I wasn't thinking about this Scripture. By God's grace I was able to let God fight for me. It was so painful to say that I forgave him but deep down I knew it was the only way to free myself. The man did not say 'sorry' or show any signs of remorse or even recognition of me. I cannot express how very painful this was. But I knew he had seen me. He knew that I remembered what he had done. Now it was time for him to carry the burden of that guilt. I will never forget what he did. But I am free from bitterness. I chose to release myself of something I was carrying around for a long time and hand it over to God.

I understand that it takes enormous courage and strength to face those who have hurt you and it may not be possible in your case to confront them as I did. It is my prayer that God will give you wisdom, peace and guidance on how to deal with situations like this in your life. God wants us to be free in every area of our lives because He loves us. Remember that God has forgiven you and He wants you to forgive those you find hardest to love. Remember Jesus' prayer for his murderers during his anguish on the cross: "'Father, forgive them, for they do not know what they are doing'" (Lk. 23:34).

8

BEING CONTENT

I know what it is to be in need, and I know what it
is to have plenty. I have learned the secret of being
content in any and every situation, … whether
living in plenty or in want. (Philippians 4:12)

Growing up in Uganda, I had so little and yet I think I was, at times, more content then than I am today. In the area I grew up in we had one thing in common: we were all poor and no one had more than the other. We didn't know any different. As an adult now living in Oxfordshire, England, I have more than I need yet feelings of contentment can be elusive. This lack of satisfaction can have a severe effect on our lives – our health, self-esteem and identity.

As humans, we can battle with low self-esteem. We are living in a generation where life is all about the surface; to the extent that we are even willing to go to extreme lengths to alter our bodies to look acceptable to society. But wait and think for a minute, you and I are created in God's image. Do we really need to change what God deems as beautiful?

I'll let you into a little secret from my teenage years. When I was fifteen years old I did not like my legs. They were shorter and smaller than those of my friends. I would daydream that if I could pull on my feet, I could simply stretch them to be longer and fatter. You see, in Uganda, for as long as I can remember, big is beautiful. Ah, if only I could wear a skirt for once and show my legs off with pride! I tried asking my friends what they thought about them, though it didn't help much. They were either painfully awkward or, being Ugandan, didn't hold back and gave me their undiluted and frank observations.

God, however, set out to eliminate this discontent for good. At the time, I attended a church that was located on the top floor of a three-storey building. I always took the lift. But on one particular day I was late and couldn't wait, so I hurried up the stairs. Halfway up, I stopped to catch my breath and saw a gentleman that I had only noticed briefly during church services. This man walked on his hands; flip-flops threaded between his fingers for protection. His legs ended below his thighs, where his knees once were. It immediately struck me that he too was taking the stairs instead of the lift. Surely if anyone was entitled to take the lift, it was him. Curious, I came up alongside him and started a conversation. He told me how he enjoyed taking the stairs from time to time because it allowed him time to pray with God in preparation for the service.

I realised in that moment that God was speaking to me. Humbled, I decided never to allow those discontented ideas about my body seep into my mind again. God is our creator and made each of our features uniquely and for a purpose – even those that we find ourselves disliking. "'Before I formed you in the womb I knew you, before you were born I set you apart'" (Jer. 1:5).

Being discontent can negatively reinforce things we have been through. For example, when I was very young, my auntie used me as a domestic slave and denied me access to school. The phrase, 'You will never become anything useful', was often slung at me. It is statements like this that I continue to battle with even now as an adult. They can make me doubt my worth and thereby disrupt my contentedness in who I am and what I am working hard at.

I have come to realise that what other people say about me does not define me but it is what God says about me in His Word that is of primary importance. God says that His grace is sufficient for me, and when I am weak, He is strong. Therefore, I am content that what He gives me is enough. "'My grace is sufficient for you, for my power is made perfect in weakness'" (2 Cor. 12:9).

God's Word instructs us to be content. You are a masterpiece, you are beautiful, and, above all else, the

God who created everything loves you. You are unique: take pride and believe this. Whatever dissatisfaction you are struggling with in your life, I pray that God will give you His perspective on you and your life in the context of His plans. Understand that God has a plan for He created you with purpose. "'For I know the plans I have for you,' declares the LORD, "plans to prosper you and not to harm you, plans to give you hope and a future'" (Jer. 29:11). It is possible that struggles with imperfection may be blinding you from seeing His designs for you. Recognize the good things He has done, and is still doing, in your life. Ask Him to show you how your struggles fit into His plan.

9

GIVING CHEERFULLY

*Remember this: Whoever sows sparingly will
also reap sparingly, and whoever sows generously
will also reap generously. Each man should give
what he has decided in his heart to give, not
reluctantly or under compulsion, for God loves a
cheerful giver. (2 Corinthians 9:6–7)*

I can confidently say that I am who I am today because
God gave so generously to me first. God giving His Son
for the sins of the world sets the precedent, an act that
should never be taken lightly. 'For God so loved the world
that he gave his one and only Son, that whoever believes
in him shall not perish but have eternal life' (Jn. 3:16). This
verse reminds me that whatever I possess in life is simply not
so important in comparison to God's sacrifice and giving.

When I give, I often question my motive. Let's face it,
it can feel good to give and be appreciated with a 'thank

you'. But I endeavour not to give if my motive is not right. We would all feel better receiving gifts or favours from people whose motives are rooted in love or genuine concern for our situation. It should come from a place of real worship, as the Word of God says, 'But when you give to the needy, do not let your left hand know what your right hand is doing' (Mt. 6:3).

My grandmother was one of those women who God imbued with a giving heart. Although she had nothing materially to speak of, she would always find some way to give to another. Occasionally, my mother sent us out from the slums to stay with my grandmother for a short time. She lived in a village in a remote area of Uganda blanketed by lush green vegetation; a place where it was notable if a single car passed through. My grandmother lived happily in a small, windowless brick house that she prided herself on keeping immaculately tidy. Those times were the best days of our childhood; we had a chance to be just kids. We would spend from dawn until dusk playing games like tag and hide-and-seek with the local children. We would climb the tallest trees and talk to the animals as we went to fetch the water and collect firewood.

I would observe my grandmother doing the most extraordinary thing. She would always prepare the day's food well before noon and once she had swept the mud floor of her home clean, she would go to her usual spot on the dusty roadside. She would then spend hours chatting to traders who would be coming back and forth from the market, some on their bicycles, others on foot. With a keen eye she would pick out someone who looked particularly tired and quiz them, 'How far are you going? No, no, no, I insist, you simply can't go any farther without eating! Come to my home and let me give you food and drink.'

As a child, I was astonished and simply could not comprehend why she would do this. Especially on the rare days we had meat, not even to mention those glorious few special occasions she would prepare one of her chickens. We would watch on with wide and jealous eyes as the little food we had was divided even further, and this stranger would be presented with the finest of our morsels.

You see, my grandmother understood something that has taken me a long time to appreciate: this was her way of worshipping God. Although she had no money to give, she did have water and a little food to share. When I would question her actions, my grandmother would rebuke me with a smile and say, 'My child, you never know who might feed you for me tomorrow!' She gave generously of the little she had and at the same time entrusted God with the future welfare of her family knowing that God sees and maybe somebody would be kind to us one day when we were in need.

I now desire to be like my grandmother, for I have seen for myself that God indeed loves a cheerful giver and like my grandmother I hope to further God's Kingdom by being a generous giver in faith. I can see for certain that God has honoured her generosity with the many blessings that I have received since that time.

Giving is a gift from God, an enabling by his Holy Spirit, that we can extend generosity towards others as an act of worship to Him. The generosity of the people that I have been blessed to meet has helped me to become the person I am today. I could always tell that the reason behind their offerings was a selfless and genuine desire to help out in any way they could and to show me love. They demonstrated this in various ways: a kind word, sometimes food, or even a roof over my head when I needed a place to stay. These acts of giving demonstrated what God's Word encourages us to do, 'Each man should give what he has decided in his heart to give, not reluctantly or under compulsion, for God loves a cheerful giver' (2 Cor. 9:7). Each time I am the recipient of someone's generosity, it amplifies my determination to worship God through giving.

I remember living with a family who hosted me in their home for a time while I was completing my studies. They were so giving that I don't think they even realised when they were doing it. One of the moments that will stay with me for the rest of my life is the act of kindness the lady of that house showed me.

Due to my constant worrying about my siblings in Africa I struggled with my academic life. I was visibly under so much stress and strain; as a result I started to suffer severe panic attacks. I remember one night in particular when this kind lady came to me; she must have heard me struggling from the hallway, and she gave freely of her time. She sat with me through midnight into the early hours, comforting me and praying for me. Slowly the panic subsided and I was eventually blessed to get some sleep. Her generosity and kindness overwhelmed my heart. She didn't have to do what she did, but she chose to do it anyway; her actions were not merely actions of charity just to make me feel better but acts of worship serving God.

There are times when our giving will feel like a burden, especially if we are sacrificially giving material things, like money, to people who are ungrateful. Please do not be discouraged but continue cheerfully in line with what God has called you to do; for the Lord who watches knows your heart and will reward your good deeds. 'Command them to do good, to be rich in good deeds, and to be generous and willing to share. In this way they will lay up treasure for themselves as a firm foundation for the coming age, so that they may take hold of the life that is truly life' (1 Tim. 6:18–19).

I want to encourage you to always pray for opportunities to bless someone else through giving – be it your time, money, smile, prayer or lending a hand in any way possible – because it pleases God. And it is good for the giver: the beauty in giving cheerfully is hard to express with words, but the feeling of fullness experienced in the heart during this act of worship is unparalleled.

10

THE POWER OF GRATITUDE

*Give thanks to the L*ORD*, for he is good.* His love
endures for ever. *(Psalm 136:1)*

How often do we concentrate our energies and attention on the negative aspects of things and forget the positive? Out of ten events, one bad thing may happen that overshadows the other nine good ones.

We all live busy lives, and some of us wake up and immediately start worrying about the day and how every part of it will progress. The challenge that we face here is in not being able to pause and be grateful for that day; the air we breathe, the family and friends in our lives. Awful events do happen in the world, but by God's grace, most of us can be thankful that we have a roof over our heads, food to eat and, by God's grace, a life to live.

The Word of God encourages us to be thankful in every situation. The term 'every situation' may not appeal to most of us because usually we express gratitude when something positive has happened to us, and only then. In Thessalonians 5:18, we are encouraged to give thanks in every situation for it is God's will. Our courage in carrying out this directive reveals our faith that God is greater than our problems.

Living by the principle of being grateful for what I have been through, both pleasant and unpleasant, has carried me through life. I never forget the days I did not have enough to eat or did not have a home to live in. Yet I was grateful that I was alive.

I have also learnt that the gift of gratitude comes with a responsibility: that of sharing in order to further the Kingdom of God. God so generously gave us His son to die for our sins to save us (Jn. 3:16). As Christians, the more we understand about this sacrificial giving, the more we will want to freely give ourselves, whether it is time, money or material possessions to name a few. We have the choice to share what was given to us with others. In doing so, we are spreading the good news of God's love for us all.

Living out the knowledge of these truths is life transforming. In the past, I never wanted to have anything nice in case people judged me for owning material things. The more God blessed me, the more uncomfortable I felt. So I went to God in prayer about feeling this way and He challenged me and taught me about the power of gratitude.

One of the things God has blessed me with is our home. Living in a beautiful and peaceful village, I sometimes feel in awe and undeserving of such a privilege. Yet I know that the way we ended up here was a miracle and a testimony that I so often share. As I enjoyed the beauty and peace of this place, I also realised that I made excuses every time someone commented that I lived in a beautiful place. While praying one day, the Lord showed me that my home, and the area I live in, are His blessings. He wanted to show me that He stands by His Word. When the apostle Paul said 'And my God will meet all your needs according to his glorious riches in Christ Jesus' (Phil. 4:19), he knew what he was talking about. Paul wasn't ashamed of the financial gifts the church sent him but instead, he counted it as a blessing from God that helped him to continue God's work. Reading this passage gave me great confidence and reassurance that I too should not be ashamed of the things God has blessed me with. Just like me, Paul had known both poverty and wealth; he found gratitude in the generosity of other Christians and in the riches of his relationship with Christ. Paul's big source of gratitude was Christ Himself, no matter what situation he was in.

When I acknowledged that these blessings were from God, I asked Him how I could best enjoy them His answer was clear and simple. He said, 'express your gratitude by sharing with others'. To that end, for those of you who know me, you will know that when it comes to sharing whatever I can, I go all out. For example, I am known for going over the top to make sure my guests are fed and made comfortable in every way possible.

When I was a young girl, my grandmother would often say to me, 'Saying "thank you" does not cost you anything and it will add to your life'. This did not mean a lot to me at the time but as I got older, I realised the importance and the meaning of gratitude.

I clearly remember the kindness of the church I attended in Kampala, where I first began to learn about Christianity. They went out of their way to support me in a time of need even though my faith was only just blossoming. After the service on Sundays they sent me home with meals for my family, even though they knew the rest of my family had no interest in attending. I was utterly horrified at my stepfather's attitude. He would always push past us to be the first to feed, greedily gorging himself. We would watch on – our bellies aching from hunger – until he was finished, leaving us the scraps to eat. I would then witness him gleefully cursing the church in the face of their generosity, believing he had duped fools into taking over his responsibilities. In contrast to him, I was eternally grateful for the church's charity. It is no understatement to say they saved my mother, my sisters and myself from starvation at that time. Moreover, my faith was reinforced: this God truly was real. As I continued to go to church, my conviction grew and I was astonished to fully understand how Christ had given his life for us, taking our place on the cross for our sins.

I am so thankful to God for the many empathetic people he has gifted me as I journey through life and for all the compassion that has been shown to me. When we are grateful we are acknowledging God's work in our lives and thanking Him. We will not always have it easy, but we will always have God on our side.

It is therefore my prayer that you are always able to look at the positive side of things. May you be grateful for who you are now and the person that you are becoming. May you be grateful for what you have and what you dream of having, for you serve a faithful God who rewards a grateful heart. Above all, may you be grateful for the gift of eternal life, bought through Christ's death for our salvation, and a new, right relationship with God.

11

WALKING IN OBEDIENCE

And this is love: that we walk in obedience to
his commands. As you have heard from the
beginning, his command is that you walk in love.
(2 John 1:6)

What comes to your mind when you think of obedience? Following a lot of rules? To me obedience is the love, acknowledgement and respect I have for God. If it is all these things then, in our own lives, we should continually examine whether we are actually obeying God. Are we being patient enough; trusting His Word and adhering to His commandments? In my experience, obedience to God is the key to unveiling the treasures He has in store for us.

Not having had an easy upbringing, I was so determined to raise my own children surrounded by love. I feared them being exposed to feelings of rejection or desertion and was anxious that we should be their primary caregivers in their early years. I would pray to God to make a way where my husband or I would be fully available to look after the children at home. But in this day and age, where both parents often need to work to make ends meet, this seemed like wishful thinking. I was, however, challenged by the Word of God when it said, "'Present your case,' says the Lord. "Set forth your arguments," says Jacob's King' (Is. 41:21).

I presented my case to God and I pleaded with Him to make a way but only according to His Will. I waited on the Lord. I remember God clearly saying to me that my prayers had been answered and it was now possible for us to look after our children in the way we desired. I thought I heard wrong so I asked Him how this would work. The answer was simple: by listening in obedience to what He said. This did not make sense to me at all, but I had to trust God's judgment.

Through prayer, I began to strongly feel that my husband had to leave his workplace at the time. I rebuked these thoughts. Really, I asked? 'Yes!' God answered by putting the same conviction on my heart each time I prayed. I continued to pray and wait on the Lord, but the answer was still the same. So, I decided to discuss it with my husband and to my amazement, he confirmed to me that he was thinking the same thing.

When we both realised this was God speaking, we chose to obey. He left his job by faith. In obedience to God,

I applied for work and received an offer that very week of a part-time job as a Learning Assessor with the organisation I had been doing some training with. Although this was not exactly what I was praying for, it was God's way of providing. It meant that we had enough finances coming in as we waited on the Lord.

My husband became self-employed and we shared the childcare of our toddlers together. This was without a doubt the answer to my prayers I had been hoping for. To give my children a stable home, with parents who were present and engaged with them and also able to provide for their material needs.

Through this process, I learnt that obedience requires listening: two years of praying, reading the Word of God, and listening to hear God answer our prayers. Revelation 14:12 calls believers to be patient, endure and remain faithful in Christ. To affirm that God was in our situation, at the end of those two years, He faithfully provided all we needed, including tools and opportunities for my husband and me to start a business.

Obedience requires us to trust in Him and sometimes it may mean enduring situations we do not like. Knowing that God is in charge makes the uncomfortable periods bearable.

After working as an Assessor for a few months, I knew it was time to move on. But I refused to listen because I was worried it would force us to go into debt. I could not see where God was taking us. I was frustrated and asked God what to do. His answer was to leave and yet I couldn't bring myself to do so. Again, I asked. How would we make ends meet and not become a burden for others? But God had spoken, and my stubbornness resulted in discipline. You see the longer I stayed in that position, the more miserable I became. So I submitted to God and handed my notice in; I had taken the leap of faith. 'He replied, "Blessed rather are those who hear the word of God and obey it"' (Lk. 11:28).

In my last year of undergraduate studies, I had difficulty raising funds for my tuition. The sponsorship I had been receiving up until that point was no longer able to help me any further and at that point my future was unclear. I could not see a way forward, but God gave me courage to trust Him to make a path for me.

A charity called Rafiki Thabo Foundation had heard of my story. The charity was offering to pay half of the amount required for my final year. This was the first I had heard of Rafiki, but I then put the dots together and realised I had known one of the charity's directors for a number of years. I was humbled by God's provision through him.

This gentleman later shared with me the story of how he started the charity. As a teenager he had taken a gap year and decided to spend some time in Africa. While there, he was very touched by the poverty of the people he had lived amongst, especially seeing the struggles young families endured. He observed how young people his own age had few options with little hope of continuing their education the way he had. He was convinced that if they were given the opportunity of further education it could enable them to better support themselves and their communities. He suddenly felt a responsibility to help source this aid for those who needed it.

Upon his return home to England, he stepped out in faith to set up the charity. He did not know how (and if) it was going to be possible to achieve his aim but he knew that he wanted to obey God's directive and so he acted and trusted that God would guide him. From a modest beginning, a single person with a burning conviction, God has honoured his commitment; Rafiki Thabo Foundation has grown from strength to strength and now faithfully supports hundreds of students throughout their higher education across East Africa.

Pondering his story, I realised that at the time of receiving God's call, he would have been scared and doubtful whether he was capable of achieving real change. He could have asked himself how it would all benefit him. Instead, by looking beyond personal gains and benefit, he heard God's call, and although he was still very young at the time, he obeyed and God has blessed his work. You and I can be like this: listen for God's voice, acknowledge His Will and in obedience carry out His work and see how it blesses others tenfold. 'This is how we know that we love the children of God: by loving God and carrying out his commands. This is love for God: to obey his commands' (1 Jn. 5:2–3).

When we obey God, we are showing that we trust Him to guide every area of our lives. I believe acting in obedience moves God's fatherly heart. He wants us, His children, to walk in loving obedience with Him and in doing so, we demonstrate the love that He desires from us.

I pray with hope that you can be encouraged by my experiences and will choose to trust God's Word and step forward in obedience to it – even when that is hard. I pray that in doing so – and as God speaks to you – your light will shine so that you will be a blessing to many.

12

STRENGTH AT THE CROSSROADS

"For I know the plans I have for you," declares
the Lord, "plans to prosper you and not to
harm you, plans to give you hope and a future."
(Jeremiah 29:11)

The future is definitely bright if we trust God, but does that mean we forget all the tough things that have happened to us in the past? Well, God gives us a choice. We either move on by faith looking forward to enjoying the blessings He has in store for us. Or, we can choose to stay where we are, dwelling on the difficult past; letting bitterness and sadness consume us.

At the age of twenty-two, I found myself at this crossroads. To the world around me I was this smiley, happy, young woman. But on the inside, I was a sad soul looking for answers, feeling all the injustice I had had to endure for years. Here in England I was living a life I never dreamt I would. I had just completed my first degree and could hardly believe it. Yes me, the girl orphaned from the slums of Kampala, who once slept on the streets and had been routinely denied the most basic education; that girl had gone on to succeed at university! Here I was; God had remembered me. He had seen all the ill-treatment and suffering I had endured but He had also seen my yearning to survive.

You see, when we go through suffering in life, it does not mean that God has forgotten us or turned away from us. It rather means that God can see the bigger picture. He sees what we are going through; He knows how much we desire for things to improve. But God calls on us to remember the good things He has done for us too.

In the book of Genesis in the Old Testament I read about a man called Jacob. He was not perfect. He persuaded his older twin brother Esau to sell his birthright in return for some homemade stew and tricked his elderly father into believing that he was actually Esau in order to obtain his father's blessing. When Jacob later suffered injustice himself, he remembered God as the Mighty God of his grandfather Abraham, and he recalled the things God had done in the past. He knew that the same great and powerful God was fighting for him and that God's promises to his family were still true.

In Genesis 33, having cheated, stolen and fled from Esau, Jacob was about to come face to face with him again – and he was scared. But when Esau, who had every right to be angry, finally caught up with his brother Jacob, at a major crossroad of decision, he chose forgiveness and a new start. 'But Esau ran to meet Jacob and embraced him; he threw his arms around his neck and kissed him. And they wept' (Gen. 33:4). This is also a wonderful picture of what God does with us, he reaches out to us where we are, embraces us and forgives us (see Lk. 15:11–32).

As I stood still and remembered everything I had gone through, I also reflected on how faithful God had been, how He protected me and how He had provided for me. Like Jacob, I could see how God had sustained me, even through hardships; how my story was *His* story. God does not forget us even when we may forget him. This gave me strength.

And yet, standing at the crossroads of my life, I found myself very happy to be where I was, but sad for what had happened to me as a child. Like Jacob, I was embarrassed and ashamed of my background. I did not want people to know about it. Many times I invented and played the part of a different person to who I was – and this would just make me sadder. I prayed about my situation and as I looked for inspiration in the Bible, I came across the story of a woman named Esther and things suddenly started to make sense.

Esther did not have the best start in life with both her parents dying, leaving her to be raised as an orphan by her uncle Mordecai. The King of Persia sought a wife from amongst the whole nation and Esther found favour with him. She married him and she was made Queen. She could have chosen to enjoy her newfound privileged life but with the help of her uncle she understood that it was God who had brought her into this position and therefore, she had a duty to follow His guidance to save the Jewish people. It must have taken Esther so much courage to admit to the King she was not Persian but that she was really an outsider of Jewish descent. We see her standing strong and trusting God to be with her. She knew she had the power and position to save the people by God's grace. As her uncle says, "'who knows but that you have come to royal position for such a time as this?'" (Esth. 4:14).

Like Esther – and like Esau when he caught up with Jacob – I had a decision to make. To either stay where I was – bitter – or move on in hope. I chose to enjoy the opportunities God has given me to further His Kingdom by sowing seeds of hope and positivity. My childhood story is a sad one, I know; but I choose to use it to lift and encourage others. To know that God knows and sees our struggles, He has a plan and it is a good plan for us.

At the crossroads we see where we have been, we know where we are, but we are not sure of what is ahead. This is how life is, and though it is scary, it is comforting to know that God will help us navigate the trials on the way. God does not want us to forget the past (there is much to be learned and understood from it), but He really wants us to use – and enjoy – the *now* and have hope for the future.

"Remember the former things, those of long ago;
I am God, and there is no other;
I am God, and there is none like me.
I make known the end from the beginning,
from ancient times, what is still to come.
I say: My purpose will stand,
and I will do all that I please."

(Isaiah 46:9–10)

A PRAYER FOR YOU

Father God,

I thank you for the opportunity to share my testimonies and experiences with your people. I pray that you will bless the individual reading this book today. I ask that your Holy Spirit stays close to them and that your Word speaks to them.

I pray that this book will be a source of encouragement always, and most especially when your children find themselves in situations where they need to trust your Word more.

I pray in the name of our Lord Jesus Christ.

Amen.

GRATITUDE

To my family: thank you for always walking with me and supporting me on this journey of faith. A special thank you to my darling husband Andrew for the endless support and wisdom.

Thank you Mike and Marietta Woods, Kathie and Mark Burbridge, Keith Landen, Margaret and Peter Beard, Susan and Ian Sydenham, Rhiannon Wong, Carly West, Martha and Fraser Lindsay, Esther and Ed Harnett, Hannah and Phil Charles, Sara Martin, Lore and John Uglow and Charlotte Burch Osborn for playing major roles in the journey of my faith.

To Hannah Morrell, I am so thankful to God for bringing us back in touch again. Your friendship, prayers, and editorial help while working on this book has been God sent.

Thank you to Lucy Warriner for your wisdom and time in copyediting and proofreading this book.

Thank you to my Bible study group for keeping me positive and focused on God's Word. You are all wonderful warriors of God.

Thank you to the Almighty God for the family He has given me all over the world and for the gift of life.

CONTACT

If you would like to get in contact with me, please choose one of the following ways:

Website: www.lelaburbridge.com
Email: lela@lelaburbridge.com
Facebook: @lelaburbridge
Instagram: @lelanburbridge
Twitter: @lelaburbridge

My memoir *Lela: Ashes of Childhood*
(ISBN: 978-1-5272-4273-9) is available
to purchase now on Amazon and in
bookshops internationally.

May the stories I share in this book be encouraging to you in you journey of life. Remember there is alway hope and love is every thing.

With love,

Lela X